SEVEN SIMPLE SPIRITUAL SECRETS TO SUCCESS AND ABUNDANCE

By MIKE BHANGU

BBP
Copyright 2021

Copyright © 2021 by Mike Bhangu.

This book is licensed and is being offered for your personal enjoyment only. It is prohibited for this book to be re-sold, shared and/or to be given away to other people. If you would like to provide and/or share this book with someone else, please purchase an additional copy. If you did not personally purchase this book for your own personal enjoyment and are reading it, please respect the hard work of this author and purchase a copy for yourself.

All rights reserved. No part of this book may be used or reproduced or transmitted in any manner whatsoever without written permission from the author, except for the inclusion of brief quotations in reviews, articles, and recommendations. Thank you for honoring this.

ISBN: 978-1-77481-065-1 (Paperback), 978-1-77481-066-8 (Hardcover), 978-1-77481-067-5 (Electronic book).

Published by BB Productions
British Columbia, Canada
thinkingmanmike@gmail.com

TABLE OF CONTENTS

Introduction

Method 1

Method 2

Method 3

Method 4

Method 5

Method 6

Method 7

Conclusion

INTRODUCTION

My name is Mike Bhangu. I've spent over twenty years studying world theologies and the many saints of the world. Through this short book, I share seven spiritual practices designed to help an individual gain success and abundance.

The fundamental principle behind the different notions presented herein is that all cause supposedly occurs in the spiritual realm and then manifests in the physical realm. The objective of these techniques is to influence the spiritual realm so to bring about desired physical changes, such as a larger home or a better career.

The notions presented are not original to me and they are those of the spiritual teachers. Take them for what you will. If you feel adventurous, give them a try. Perhaps there's something to these ancient techniques. Perhaps they'll help you gain the success and abundance you desire.

METHOD 1

Step 1 of this method asks that an individual write down the things that he or she desires, adding or removing from the list as one progresses.

Step 2. Read the list three times daily—once in the morning, once at noon, and once at night. Provide more detail to each want as you progress.

Step 3. Think about the list as often as possible.

Step 4. Speak not to others about your list and speak only to your inner power (the Holy Spirit). This inner power will unfold to your mind the method to realizing the items on the list.

If a new desire arises, write it down, and if one wishes to remove an item, this is okay.

When the wants on the list manifest, be grateful and thank your inner power (the Holy Spirit) and The Source.

Note that to break habits and gain good health are harder to accomplish through this method and the other methods. Choose easier wants such as money, house, car, etc.

METHOD 2

This method requires 30 days to practice.

Step 1. State the goal. For example, a new car. Write this goal on a card. Stress not about how the goal will be achieved. The answers will come to you.

Step 2. Whenever possible, in a day, read the card. Do this for 30 days. As a minimum, look at the card every morning and every night. Moreover, think of the goal joyously and positively, from a calm state of mind, and from all angles. Be mindful of emotions, as they too must be joyous and positive.

While exercising this method, rise above narrow-mindedness and do not think about fears and worries. Replace fear and worry with the positive goal, and surround the self with positivity—positive people, books, music, conversations, and so on.

Step 3. Take action and do not sit about. In particular, when a reasonable idea enters the time and space of thought. Act on your ideas. Every person has a right to abundance.

Step 4. Serve humanity. The Source helps those who help others.

While practicing this method, take control of the mind and thoughts. Stay positive. In addition, each day, do more than is required of you.

If your goal comes about, be grateful and thank The Source, for all comes from The Source, and help those who require help.

METHOD 3

Method 3 is more for those seeking an answer to a question.

Step 1. Before falling asleep, visualize a picture frame. Within this frame, visualize the question to which an answer is required.

Supposedly, the answer will come to you within the next few days.

METHOD 4

This method requires 3 days to practice.

Step 1. After attaining a meditative state, with your eyes still closed, focus your attention between the eyebrows and visualize a small light. Within this light, visualize the object of desire.

Step 2. Practice step 1 for three days, adding detail to the object each time.

Step 3. After three days of practice, forget about the object of desire. The Cosmos will then act.

As always, when a desire comes about, be grateful and show that gratitude by helping others.

METHOD 5

This method isn't as simple as the others, as it requires a person to enter the Astral Plane. Supposedly, we all enter the Astral Plane during sleep. While in this plane of existence, create what is desired. This can be done by influencing the subconscious to project what is desired. The subconscious can be influenced by bombarding the mind with information, and in this case, pertinent to the goal.

This method, as the others, suggests that all cause is first in the spiritual realm, and what we have in the physical realm is the effect.

METHOD 6

Inner peace and joy attract abundance, and this is because inner peace and joy are Godly and abundance comes from God.

Step 1. Attain a peaceful and joyous meditative state. While attaining this state, meditate on the energy located by the heart, and focus your attention between the brows.

Step 2. After achieving a meditative state, thank The Source for what you have.

Step 3. Ask The Father/The Source to teach that The Source is the power behind all wealth and the value within all things.

Step 4. State: I and The Father are one.

The ideas and opportunities will arrive. Receive the ideas and opportunities, and remain in a state of joy and peace. Remember to thank The Source and to give some of what you earn to help humanity.

METHOD 7

Of all the methods, I particularly enjoy method 7, as this technique appears to increase an individual's luck.

This method requests that a person chant the Mool Mantra 108 times daily. There is no prescribed limit to the number of days an individual must practice this method, or sessions in a day. I've discovered that more one is able to repeat this mantra, the better life experiences become. The Mool Mantra is as follows:

Ik. Onkar. Sat Naam. Kartaa Purakh. Nirbhau. Nirvair. Akaal Moorat. Ajooni Saibhang. Gurprasad. Jap. Aad sach. Jugaad sach. Hai bhee sach. Nanak hose bhee sach.

"**Ik**: There is ONE (Ik) reality, the origin and the source of everything. The creation did not come out of nothing. When there was nothing, there was ONE, Ik.

Onkar: When Ik becomes the creative principal it becomes Onkar. Onkar manifests as visible and invisible phenomenon. The creative principle is not separated from the created—it is present throughout the creation in an unbroken form, 'kaar'.

Sat Naam: The sustaining principle of Ik is Sat Naam, the True Name.

Kartaa Purakh: Ik Onkar is Creator (Purakh) and Doer (Kartaa) of everything.

Nirbhau: That Ik Onkar is devoid of any fear, because there is nothing but itself.

Nirvair: That Ik Onkar is devoid of any enmity, because there is nothing but itself.

Akaal Moorat: That Ik Onkar is beyond Time (Akaal) and yet exists.

Ajooni: That Ik Onkar does not condense and come into any birth. All the phenomenon of birth and death of forms are within it.

Saibhang: That Ik Onkar exists on its own, by its own. It is not caused by anything before it or beyond it.

Gurprasaad: That Ik Onkar expresses itself through God-Manifest, known as Sat Guru (Holy Spirit). Through the Lord's grace and mercy (Prasaad) this happens."
(Source: http://www.sikhiwiki.org/index.php/Mool_Mantar)

Jap: Chant.

Aad Sach: True in the Primal Beginning.

Jugaad Sach: True throughout the different epochs.

Hai Bhee Sach: True here and now.

Nanak Hosee Bhee Sach: Forever true, says Nanak.

While chanting this mantra, focus the sound vibrations near the heart chakra and your awareness toward The Source.

The Mool Mantra was written by Guru Nanak and inspired by God's Spirit. This mantra is a brief description of The Source, and simultaneously, it reveals the nature of the cosmos.

All mantras, prayers, or music written by a truly holy person, through whom God speaks, are so because the holy individual combined specific sounds together to make celestial sentences and these sounds power-up a person's invisible presence. A strong magnetic field is the key to a good life.

A human being has two natures, the physical and the subtle, and the latter can be influenced by sounds and vibrations. Since the physical and the subtle are interrelated, a change in the invisible component of a person naturally influences the physical half of a human.

Everything in existence was first conceptualized by The Great Architect. Then it manifest as a metaphysical thing—spirit—blueprint. After which, the physical evolved from the subtle. Consequently, all material things exist within the parameters of their subtle essence.

Every person, thing, and place emanates a magnetic field, or what some might call an aura, and a person's magnetic field influences his or her thoughts, actions, health, luck, and the type of experiences an individual will attract. The stronger a person's aura the better and the higher degree of positivity he or she will encounter.

The Mool Mantra heightens an individual's invisible presence and this state naturally attracts heightened life experiences. In addition, as with other mantras, the Mool Mantra energizes a practitioner.

If you desire not to practice the Mool Mantra to improve the magnetic field, there are other methods. The simplest, and perhaps the most difficult, is to think and behave in accordance to the better aspects of the human condition such as love, truth, compassion, humility, and contentment. Simultaneously, ignoring the influences of the ugly half of the human such as anger, lust, attachment, selfish ego, and greed. Thinking and behaving as such creates a vibration that naturally attracts success, happiness, and abundance.

CONCLUSION

In conclusion, there's something to be said about not discussing a goal or project in progress. For some reason, when an individual speaks about a goal or project before completion, the goal or project doesn't reach fruition. So, when working toward something, keep it to yourself until realized.

Some suggest that when a person speaks about a goal, he or she releases a vibration of satisfaction, and indicates to the Cosmos that he or she has experienced what he or she is working toward, negating the actual experience of achieving the goal. Furthermore, when an individual speaks about a project in progress, this releases endorphins and provokes feelings of satisfaction, similar to when a goal is complete. This can lead to less motivation invested into a project.

Negative thoughts can also be a hinderance, and when negativity enters the time and space of thought, remind the self that The Father is the source of all thoughts and shift your awareness to the energy located by the heart.

I hope you enjoyed this short read, and if using any one of these methods you achieved your goal, please write to me and share your experience: thinkingmanmike@gmail.com. Take care.

BOOKS BY MIKE BHANGU

CPSIA information can be obtained
at www.ICGtesting.com
Printed in the USA
LVHW090804170821
695469LV00010B/1285